D0840787

Broken Butterflies

Emerging Through Grief, A Suicide
Survivor's Poetic Journal

KARISA MOORE

Published by EA Books Publishing a division of
Living Parables of Central Florida, Inc. a 501c3
EABooksPublishing.com

DEDICATION

To all who grieve, struggle, and hope in the aftermath of

depression, suicide, and loss.

God will not disappoint. He is faithful.

To my husband and children, I am grateful that we find hope,

faith, and love together,

even in our sorrow.

CONTENTS

Born a Caterpillar

Shedding Suicide

Cocoon of Circumstance

Flying with Broken Wings

ACKNOWLEDGMENTS

God, nothing is impossible for you! Thank you for transforming what the enemy meant for evil into good.

To my husband and children, you are an endless supply of joy and inspiration for my writing!

To my blog readers, what a pleasure it is to turn the page on suicide with you! You are beautiful broken butterflies that encourage and inspire me to love and write more deeply.

Thank you to my mentor, Diane, your encouragement towards publishing helped this caterpillar work through fear and prepare to become so much more.

To the EA Book Publishing team, wow! You transformed raw text into a beautiful poetic butterfly.

Cheri and Wanda, your patience and kindness helped me to remain still while in the publication cocoon. Thank you for giving me the courage to step out and share the hope of Christ through poetry.

Amanda, thank you for bringing my butterfly to life. You captured the strength and beauty of our brokenness in your illustration.

Natalie, from the word, go, you understood the poetry, the purpose, and my overarching desire to bring hope to the readers. Thank you for editing my book!

Dear Caterpillar,

My oldest son took his own life in 2014. Devastation does not begin to describe how I feel as a mother. I wrestle with questions about God, whom I choose to embrace in my grief. Can I live with the fact that He is sovereign, but mankind also has free will? Is his plan good, even when the events of our lives are not? Like the Old Testament story of Joseph, I recognize that the enemy meant my son's death for evil, but I remain wide open to God's bigger story. A story full of surprising possibilities that transform ashes into beauty.

Through submission to God's perfect will, I discover death does not have final say. Not over my son's life, nor mine. The trials you are experiencing do not end God's story. As I study scripture and glean wisdom from other survivors of depression and suicide, I see grace, love, joy, and peace abound when we stand firm in our impossible sorrows. Don't be afraid to wrestle with God. His ways are not our own. It is in embracing the fullness of God's character we find He is untamably good.

Becoming what God intends does not exempt me – or you, dear reader – from the difficulties life brings. Predators remain. Life is fragile. We may emerge a broken butterfly, but oh how others take note of God's love and mighty power when we fly in our brokenness.

Are you cocooned in similar circumstances? Do you long to emerge a butterfly who trusts God fully? There are four stages of a butterfly: egg, larva, pupa, and adult. Like the life cycle of a butterfly, grief can be transformed into unexpected beauty.

May the poetry collected from my first three years of grieving offer hope, inspire and challenge you. We share familiarity in grief. Trust His provision, faithfulness, love, and perfect plan. Even if the wounds of this life seem to render flight impossible, I testify . . . you will fly in God's strength.

Expect life to emerge from the cocoon of circumstances wrapped around you now. Grow still in the waiting. God is transforming us into beautiful butterflies who inspire others to fly with wings broken by depression.

Sincerely,

A Beautiful Broken Butterfly

Journaling

Just as I recorded the transformation of grief to broken butterfly, you have the opportunity to journal in the margins or at the end of each section. My poems come out of observing others, nature, scripture, and my own struggle. I found provision, promise and protection in grief through walks, new journeys, connections with family and friends. Even when I feel like closing off from the world, I have a few foundational tools that keep me moving forward. Meditation on scripture, writing, hiking, and photography get me unstuck when I start to grow stagnant.

As you read, discover core habits that you can practice and integrate. Observe and record your thoughts, questions, and scriptures. The poems themselves might trigger questions or thoughts or you can pick from the list included here.

1. What are your fears? For family? Friends? What are three simple scriptures to speak over those fears?

2. Create new memories: Make a list of 2-3 things you would like to do in honor of your loved one. Is there a special birthday event you could do every year?

3. How are you caring for your physical needs? Grief takes a lot out of the body. Hydrate, even if you can't eat. What are three things that you will commit to doing for your body, even when you don't feel like completing the task?

4. Social events can be difficult, but important to attend. Create a simple exit plan. How long will you stay? What events might be too much? Have some friends in place to help you if you look overwhelmed.

5. Emotions are all over the place in grief. Becoming aware

of and identifying today's feelings aid in healing. Emotions are tools of connection not weapons. What are you feeling today? What does God say about those emotions? Create a short poem (Haiku for example: 5-7-5 syllable lines) about today's grief.

6. I found that I could not look too far ahead without becoming overwhelmed. What do you think "give us today our daily bread" (Matthew 6:11) means in grief? How has God provided for you today?

7. Begin noticing provision in nature. How are the animals and flowers cared for? Record observations using your five senses.

8. Exercise is an excellent habit, supplying energy for your grief taxed body, and giving fresh oxygen to the mind. List three goals such as a regular 10-minute walk, hike at the park with friends, or a trip to the gym. Make one fun long-term goal to accomplish with friends.

9. Laughter is such good medicine. Tears and laughter are companions; we often switch back and forth easily between the two. Make up jokes with your kids, go see your favorite comedian. Record a funny event or saying. How is laughter helping you?

10. Where is your quiet space? It is okay to get away for a bit. Create a simple sanctuary to praise and worship with uplifting music.

11. Worship and fellowship puts us in an excellent position as we grieve. We can encourage others, pray, sing, and grow in God's word. What is God teaching you in your grief? How can you encourage someone else who is struggling? Can you share your grief?

Surrender Your Wings

Surrender is not a wound rendering your wings useless,

But the gift from God, lifting you to His highest purpose.

Isaiah 61:1-4 (NIV) *The Spirit of the Sovereign Lord is on me, because the Lord has anointed me to proclaim good news to the poor. He has sent me to bind up the brokenhearted, to proclaim freedom for the captives and release from darkness for the prisoners, to proclaim the year of the Lord's favor and the day of vengeance of our God, to comfort all who mourn, and provide for those who grieve in Zion – to bestow on them a crown of beauty instead of ashes, the oil of joy instead of mourning, and a garment of praise instead of a spirit of despair. They will be called oaks of righteousness, a planting of the Lord for the display of his splendor.*

Born a Caterpillar

The fragile reality of humanity is, because of the fall, we are all born into a crawling, caterpillar-like state of depression.

The question is: Do we become butterflies?

Genesis 3:9-10 (ESV) *But the LORD God called to the man and said to him, "Where are you?" And he said, "I heard the sound of you in the garden, and I was afraid, because I was naked, and I hid myself."*

Death Touched Butterfly

Cocooned.

Wings folded

into cramped quarters of fragile purpose.

Too young.

Death touched you,

ripped your still-forming chrysalis,

Forced wings open to the dust

of humanity.

You hid,

deep within safety,

questioning the wisdom of God.

Why you?

Why did he mold you

to fly in a world chained by gravity?

Depression Ghetto

The house shivers and sighs, naked bones exposed.

Groaning against gentle breezes, wishing

collapse.

But the skeleton stubbornly holds.

Sunken eyes devoid of life stare out,

judging the world

that so cruelly neglected intended purpose.

White picket fence, the last defense from

decay, remains locked tight.

Taunting passersby with KEEP OUT.

(As if anyone wants to COME IN).

But the weary WELCOME mat still invites

… if we triple-dog dare

to know the ghost of who you could have been.

Repeating the Blues

Awkward memories belt out

like haunting blues.

Melody seeps into bones

like chilled rain.

Soul shivers to the core

like a scratched

record.

Doomed to repeat

Doomed to repeat

Depression like a needle

wearies its way

into grooves of gray.

The mantra repeats

like haunting blues

'til your being aches to

smash the record, the player,

and anything else

that reminds of unforgiven sorrows.

Pickpocket

Depression is a pickpocket,

pinching souls

of

pluck.

Sieve of Coarse Fortune (Haiku)

Suicidal thought

Straining breath from finer hope

Sieve of coarse fortune.

Ugly Duck Interrupted

"Such an ugly duckling," the others cackled, slapping the water in agreement.

(Your head ducked)

Under the burden of shameful stares.

(You swam away,)

Inclined to believe what others say.

(You)

Couldn't see the swan, swimming smooth as silk on the other side of the reeds.

(Searching)

Inside yourself for true identity.

(Your answers)

Decidedly never came.

(You)

Ended the story before your clouded reflection cleared.

To Be Continued

Didn't know I was talking to suicide.

Goodbye was not on my lips.

"See you this afternoon,"

promised more time.

Silence breathed on the line between us,

like a to-be-continued story,

never completed . . .

You hung up.

I still wait

for the afternoon to come.

Earthquaked Soul

Screams from the fissures

Of an earthquaked soul

From the crumbled cracks of a child "deceased."

No words, just the gaping maw of grief.

With equal force, the Spirit pushes back

Against caving walls of motherhood.

Opening resurrection doors

To the Father's will

That no temporary grave consumes.

Building fortified love and hope where there are no words

Just a broken heart that welcomes orphans in.

I Was Never Here

The Problem with a note left behind?

Your unique handwriting betrays

That your existence matters.

Lost to Suicide

Amid the fireworks, your little hand

slipped into crowded adulthood

before your mind developed a sense of direction.

Grasping anything to garner comfort,

But fear is a poor companion.

Absence begged me to give up on you

… but what mother can?

I attempted a missing person's report,

but was laughed out of the station.

"He's finding himself, Ma'am," the experts scoffed,

even as my happy-boy fliers faded

… amid other lost, bulletin-board souls.

The exhausted search now buried

… I grip my Daddy's hand,

so I don't lose myself in the crushing mob of grief.

Cradle of Prayer

We huddle against the odds,

battle bruised and broken,

interlocked by purpose,

cradling each other in prayer.

The Funeral (Haiku)

Minutes chase hours

Around red circles of grief

Grave opens. Comfort.

Ripe Graves (Haiku)

Graves, ripe with blossoms,

always freshly planted in

the plot of our minds.

<u>Settled Smiles</u>

I reach into photos …

attempting CPR on settled smiles.

<u>The Void of Your Presence</u>

The void of your presence

Presses hard into my thoughts today

Jumbling the jigsaw pieces

Of my fragilely framed reality.

How can I complete life's puzzle

Without you?

Open Arrangements (Haiku)

Withering flowers,

grave with misfortune. Surprise

blossoms in my soul.

Hope Snuggled Beneath Death (Haiku)

Snowflakes soothe my soul,

While silent seeds of spring drink

Snuggled beneath death.

<u>Hope Planted in the Soil of Grief</u>

Not quite a year since

you were planted

in soil that bears no fruit.

Yet I refuse a barren field.

Death digs deep

frozen seeds of potential.

I tend the garden of my grief

until winter loosens grip.

 I reap a plump harvest of hope

that thaws more souls.

Shedding Suicide

The caterpillar sheds its layers, drawing strength as it grows.

2 Corinthians 5:17 (KJV) *Therefore if any man be in Christ, he is a new creature: old things are passed away; behold, all things are become new.*

Suicide Butterfly

A wisp of beauty landed close to me.

Separate, but the same.

I marveled at its will to live.

A vibrant delicate life,

Short, yet powerful,

Because it changed me.

Tiptoeing Around the Grave

Tiptoeing around

Him,

My fragile reality etched in

Stone.

I slip into loneliness and

Remember.

Baptism of Possibility

I am impossibility,

Chained to prison bars of depression stats,

Yet singing hymns of freedom.

Rattling the gates of hell to

Open

You to the baptism of

Possibility.

A Waltz I Did Not Choose

Grief, a dance partner I did not

choose, puts me on display

for a waltz I have not learned.

He does not care

that my ankles are unlocked

or that I am unwilling

to follow his lead.

His grip is tight on my hand

and weighty on my waist.

Demanding elegance, he holds his head

with the confidence of centuries of one-two-threes.

I rise when I should fall, and fall when

I should rise.

Slowly, I realize the waltz will play on

until I follow Grief's lead.

Back right foot,

slide the left …

A repeated pattern of elegant sadness,

Until the crowd gasps in awe.

Unexpectedly, I find

joy and compassion in this

waltz I did not choose.

<u>Clocking In</u>

I didn't quit my job of loving

When you stopped punching your time card.

I clock in to life,

Heart uncalloused by the rough, 24-hour work of losing.

I freely hope, with splinters of grief digging deep into my soul.

Faith, joy and compassion embrace the world

With a work ethic that suicide cannot render unconscious

To the world around me.

Jarritos Memories

A bottle of memories

Sparkling with your laughter,

Sipped slowly by my broken heart.

Silly sombrero on your head,

Inviting life with your dimpled smile,

As cheeks puff to blow out candles.

I walk by the Mexican soda in the aisle

And you make my sorrow smile.

You Knit Motherhood

On this day

You knit motherhood into my soul.

Sweeping away cobwebs

Of brokenness and rebellion

Filling my world

With vivid colors I grew up missing.

You deepened my breath,

Made me reach deeper inside

For strength I had never explored,

Laughter never expressed,

Hope unquenchable

By death.

On this day

You made me a mother.

Not even the grave can swallow

My joy.

Dusty, Concrete Realities

Dreams – dusty realities

removing time and distance

Like a movement of dissidence,

tucked into a symphony of reason.

You – are a memory

that makes no sense,

Resurrected by heartache,

sewn together by longing.

Until – the persistent alarm

shatters my dreams

to a heavy concrete world without you.

Box of Memories

I sift the box of meaning.

Your fragrance

lingers

I boil off the excess

and let

These treasures simmer

in my soul.

I search for something missing

That never could

be boxed in.

Breathing Life into Strangers

I caught a glimpse of you,

my son,

mirrored in another teenager

standing in

your shoes,

your smock,

your hat,

ready to serve me.

"How are you?" I ask him,

emboldened by your death to

Reach into his life

that isn't yours.

Witnessing to a stranger, still

breathing, the

value of each breath.

<u>Warm Yourself in My Eyes</u>

May I sit awhile and warm my soul in your eyes? Eyes

crackling and popping with stories,

stirred by my need for hope.

Hope boasting of losses

gained and tragic victories;

Of dreams, love and faith.

Faith refusing to be dampened by despair, quiet

constant discipline battling the reality of death.

Death framing itself behind your eyes.

Eyes raised from

grave circumstances. Circumstances

snuffing out my flame! Flame now fanned

by the passionate compassion of your hope. Hope

fueling my soul with logs of endurance,

sparking life in my dimmed eyes. Eyes that others ask if they can
sit awhile,

warming their cold souls with the fire of my hope.

The Collider

Amid the darkness of hovering grief, cold

reality collides with warm consciousness, like

atoms birthing a new creation in the deep.

My Children Drew Me In

Giggles and crayons melts

the distance between our sorrow.

Sketches out souls, framed together

in a mosaic moment of

play.

I miss him

Echoes in our quiet, parallel

expressions of color.

Each grieves, uniquely

united by the unquiet outline

of our circumstances.

Gift Wrapped Grief (Haiku)

Popsicle photos

and fragrant fir trees waving

open gift-wrapped grief.

Unwrapped Sorrows

Packaged patiently within pain …

the gift of possibility.

Unopened or open

does not change content.

Bitterness and despair torn open and discarded,

a shiny exoskeleton no longer attractive.

My passion – hope secreted within the gift of sorrow.

Climbing Suicide's Crag

Rocks crumble, encouraging

gravity

to finish thought.

But truth, confident guide with gritty fingers,

secures novice climbers

reaching for impossible sunrises.

Dancing the Sanguine Blues

Forecast calls for blistering blues,

Shame soaked in a raging torrent of emotions.

I put on defiant dancing shoes,

Shape prolific pools of hopelessness into a

Holy halos of dancing rainbows.

Until bones break to life and support the

Futile flesh of my reality.

I Didn't Press Replay

I didn't press replay but there you are,

smirking in my dreams.

I search each one,

hoping to find clues.

Memories

Longings scream through the fog of grief,

I blindly reach out to hold a child not here.

Take comfort my soul.

Memories are your keepsake.

Two Lovers and a Friend: Grief Tug-of-War

Grief is two lovers yanking you in opposite directions.

The Past pulls out his photo albums, showing off his plump family of memories,

Inviting you to warm yourself by the faded fires of yesterday,

Still snapping and popping in your mind,

Until you realize you are freezing to death.

The Future pulls out his photo albums, displaying empty pockets, missing face,

Sucking you into a black hole of regret,

Threatening to crush you over and over with what will never appear.

Two lovers trying to tear you apart.

The Present stays out of the fray, content to be your

Friend, a daily companion,

Walking beside you, sustaining you,

Pulling the curtains closed on yesterday,

Introducing you to new brilliant mornings.

He holds you tightly as you sob,

Revealing the unknown in quantities you can handle,

Remaining always here with you.

The Past never stays;

The Future may never come.

Do I Really Matter?

God cupped your matter in his hands,

shaping body, soul, and mind,

breathing life into atoms.

Your worth cannot be destroyed,

only repurposed and transformed.

<u>Comforting the Comforter</u>

I comfort myself by wrapping up in the

Truth of who you were, not in the

Grief of who you thought you should be.

Let Pain Sing

When

I unlatch

the cage around

my heart, and

pull out

the throbbing

pain within,

I am

surprised to find a

small,

trembling bird, waiting

for the

strength of release.

No Regrets Mother Mary

If I could reach back and trace the pink face, not yet

troubled and embroiled in years, stroke little fingers

and nuzzle dependent heart, would it make a difference in your dying?

No.

There should be no surprise. Obeying God leads

to rolling the dice with men.

I carried complete power and total submission in my womb nine months.

But even as I nursed truth, I struggled

to die to motherhood.

The cross born of my obedience.

Your heart now beats in the tender words spoken to

the desperate and despised. We fellowship with bread offered

to empty bellies.

Our hope is planted, watered, and grows in resurrected soil.

And I breathe …

Oh, my soul breathes

deeply the fragrance of your presence with me. The cross did not

separate us. It made us one!

You live in the past, present, and future.

I find you in the gutters of obedience.

Cocoon of Circumstance

We struggle with wrapping up in becoming, the in-between places of our circumstances. But, oh, the lessons learned in becoming still and knowing God.

Luke 12: 28 (NLT) *And if God cares so wonderfully for flowers that are here today and thrown into the fire tomorrow, he will certainly care for you. Why do you have so little faith?*

Cocooned in Depression Is a Butterfly

Where's the bell to ring, to raise the alarm:

I'M NOT DEAD!

Cocooned in a casket of depression,

quickly lowering hopes

into the chasm of darkness.

Wait.

One second more.

Wait.

To stretch wings and discover

I am a born-again butterfly.

A Drop of Hope

I am but one drop in the sea of depression, but

Oh, the magnitude of one drop!

Ladder of Words

I Write a

Ladder of

Words to

Climb out

Of this pit

Of disrepair.

Inside a Suicide Mother's Locket

Suicide snapped future pictures of you.

So I open the locket of my soul wide,

Share who you were,

Not who you will be.

I traced chubby cheeks, as the rhythm

Of the rocker sang you to sleep, breathed

Deeply your baby scent.

I squealed with delight at first steps and words.

Bandaged scrapes, wiped tears and kissed bruises.

I listened to life beating hard with

Challenges no child should bear,

And ached for God to heal you inside and out.

God, I try to understand why you allowed an unfinished

Work of art to be painted into my life.

Today, I have no calls from your college dorm, no

Laughter as you burst through the door for Christmas.

No bride on your arm to swap funny stories, and

No grandchildren to cherish …

I can't quite release these things. I long

For them. I hoped for them. So, I open my heart

Wider still, until joy paints a new

Picture into the empty memories of where you should be.

Depression Is Not Meant for the Church Coatroom

I attempted to stuff depression into the racks of the church coatroom before

straightening my features into a well-pressed smile.

You, who did not hide your sorrow from your Father,

had the usher bring my cloak of despair back to me.

Shoulders drooped as I slipped into the putrid pew of religious repetition,

believing faith wasn't ready to share my coarse reality.

But scripture shook me awake. The world needs

my tears, struggle, and depression.

Believers sing the blues too.

I confess, I struggle to accept Your ways.

Bones, broken with grief, scream to give in.

You give sanctuary to my lament,

meet questions with open goodness.

I am reminded: God put on the cloak of humanity

to understand me.

So when I wear depression into the sanctuary,

It unveils an open invitation for others to be real with You.

Grammar Checking Suicide

Some punctuate life with a consistent and steady .

Some complete their lives bungee jumping with expression !

Others leave us guessing at their purpose ?

But you went out with a ;

An incomplete sentence that can no longer be edited.

Becoming a Lamp in the Darkness

I have lived in darkness,

wrapped up in the blanket of its truth.

I have smothered

hope and shut out liars

who offered to light my way with burnt-out

candles of philosophy.

I thought I had insulated

myself from darkness by embracing its *truth*.

Nothing begets nothing.

We're all dead anyway.

Until

fear had mastered my taste buds, and my

craving had birthed bitterness.

I begged death to

swallow me whole. It did.

Soul-crushing pain that I could

never quite medicate out of existence.

Death became my hope.

But a pesky light persisted,

It didn't care if I trusted. The warmth of its glow stayed constant

when others faded away. Like an inn at the end of a long

journey, it offered rest from

my aching confusion.

The lantern brought me from the woods

of my tangled shadows.

Secure in its source,

in its never-changing nature,

a humble truth never experienced in my boasting,

darkness of doubt. It didn't demand I believe, nor

did it exact the price of darkness. It paid

in full every

debt I owed. This light didn't scramble as I did,

to snuff out pain. It bore it. Willingly.

It hung in the darkness for me.

I had never experienced such light.

A state of being, rather than doing, a love

that pursues

rather than playing hide-and-seek.

My soul caught fire as I warmed by the fire

of its glory.

I am a light to you in the darkness

Inviting warmth and freedom to the darkest souls.

<u>Hope in Our Cell of Circumstances</u>

Night defiantly whispers,

"No rest here." Sleep

steals the covers,

tauntingly tapping tick-tock

on your brain.

Scripture unfolds like a father's

bedtime story to his child,

like a mother's lullaby.

Remembered promises,

experienced and witnessed, repeat hope

in the cell of circumstances,

fluff pillows and prepare the heart

to receive just enough.

God tucks the soul

beneath the blanket of his wings

and feeds truth and comfort, though

our fallen bodies fail us.

Testament Grit

Evidence of grit:

Heels dug into turf

in repetitive resilience.

Battered souls

wilted weary

by devastating defeats,

coached back up

to the surprise of

of our enemy's doggedness.

Shoulders pressed forward

against all odds.

Hope faithfully

gains ground, with eyes

firmly fixed on the end zone

of belief.

Penny Poems

I deposit poems

like pennies into

the bank of your soul.

Crack open when

you need to splurge

on hope.

Aired Out

Sucking in the stale air

of depression, regurgitating

regret day after day.

Throw open windows!

You break the seal of

our tomb of circumstances.

Resurrect the fresh fragrance

of hope planted in the sunshine of our dreams.

Filter life through the curtains of our mourning soul

Invite us to

open our eyes to Spring.

Grief on the Grill

Marinated memories tenderized by time,

simmer and sizzle with laughter on the grill.

Still tender pink and moist with grief.

Yet ... each bite bursting with the fresh flavor of hope.

Mountaintop Corner Office

A glory glimpse of your mighty work, after grunting and groaning

up mounds of sweaty mountains – so worth

the breathing room of the corner office. I knew you here.

Studied and learned to read the blueprints of your plan for my life.

Returning to the valley assembly line ...

I quickly reverted into a disgruntled, blue-collar drone.

Clocking in complaints among the hot rows of trouble.

The boss, distant and irrelevant to the idols

cluttering my desk. I missed our team-building exercises.

So daily I rise early, hike the heights for a clearer view of your presence with me.

Thanksgiving—The WD-40 of Faith

Thankfulness is my WD-40.

When worked into my frame,

I remember Your goodness.

You built a firm foundation of

faith, hope, and love.

No matter the damage I withstand,

I can count on the sturdiness of my God.

Working Out in God's Gym

Suicide doesn't water down faith with

flowery prose about God.

Take doubts to the mat and wrestle

with who you believe Him to be.

Depression is the resistance between

His will and yours being done.

Sacrifice, daily dripping with sweat,

works out belief on the gym floor of reality.

Muscles cry out at the strain of discipline.

But still He coaches beyond what

you think you can reach. *Just one more breath!*

Shaping and toning your soul into His image.

Turning heads with a foxy endurance

that is not of this world!

Grief Sings

I sing when the horn

Of victory is faint with grief.

Belief is the miracle melody,

Harmonizing with heaven.

Prayer Closet

There is a secret staircase I

spiral down, when the front

stairs feel too exposed. In

the darkness of fledgling hours,

I retreat. Tracing your love notes

with heart, soul, and mind. Sipping

the earthy tea of your testaments. Conversing

together as old friends. Turning over to you all that I am.

Allowing sunrise to color in the black-and-white outline

of your form. Loving because you first loved me.

Love: The Hand Scarred for Me

You woke me from the terror of my nightmares,

Said I was worth your time, your pain, your cross.

You didn't shy away from my stains,

From the sorrow I could not repay.

You awoke my desire,

A fire for something

Beyond self,

Beyond limit,

Beyond fear.

You lit

My

Path

Until I

Became You,

Holding out my scarred hands,

Lightening another soul's nightmare.

Flying with Broken Wings

God became a caterpillar for us, to show us we can be

transformed.

Philippians 2: 5-7 (Berean Study Bible) *Let this mind be in you which*

was also in Christ Jesus: Who, existing in the form of God, did not

consider equality with God something to cling to, but emptied Himself,

taking the form of a servant, being made in human likeness.

Redemption Butterflies

When I gaze too long at the hard shell of the grave,

I despair without your physical presence.

When I rubberneck the collision of God and man on the cross,

I am overwhelmed by the required suffering sin must pay.

But

When I fix my eyes upon the reality of resurrection,

Your authority surges through my veins!

I testify, the cracked grave and crude cross

the transforming chrysalis,

Where redemption butterflies emerge!

God's Tattoo

I etched part of my story into my arms, temporary

tattoos of my brokenness that time will fade, but You ...

You hammered my personhood into your hands

for eternity.

On the Cliff

Depression stares out at the endless sea of unknown dangers

drowning in despair.

Hope gazes intently across the vast waters

expecting to discover new land.

Stumbling Through Depression

When You brush the canvas black,

And my vision can't penetrate the opacity

of your masterpiece, shadows of sorrow thicken.

Still, you paint over my doubts with sunrises.

Nitty-Gritty Love

Love that sweats, pours

out humility, serves

like it's goin' out of style.

Love that callouses,

but isn't calloused, that

gets dirt under its nails, when

everyone else washes their hands

of you.

Love that endures

the scars of loss,

hangs on in darkness, when

others hang loose in light times.

Love that climbs into pits, pulls

us from flames and washes our wounds.

Nitty-gritty love that removes royal robes to know

the dust of our humanity!

Pregnant Scripture

Cradled within the womb of death, scripture beats defiant.

Lean in to discern hope's unfolding;

Multiplying cells of truth over pregnant centuries.

Giving breath to us, Too often, dragged to the grave.

Soothing empty arms,

with strong proof of life after life.

So soft, thundering in the vast

noise of doubt's marketplace.

Firming

backbone to bow

to no man.

Resolving who knit whom together.

Renewing covenant with an empty

grave.

Our souls

swollen with

grief – for but a while.

Christian Tomb Raider

Hope lit in abstract, easily

snuffed out by passionate loneliness.

Attempts to breathe, clotted by

veins scarred by sorrow.

Eyes, scaled by experience.

Belief, closed in sleep against the cruelties

of the world.

I'm not afraid to climb into the ditch with you.

I've dug this grave before.

Grave digger turned grave robber.

Joined, a band of brothers and sisters saturated

in the oil of faith.

Searching, tombs of darkness for a pulse because you matter.

To me.

Torch of souls, leaning close to

living corpses already making beds of graves.

Relentless, calling Lazarus from the

tomb.

It is not your time yet.

I am hope, concrete with dirty fingers.

Jesus' Cologne

Breathe in the sweet fragrance of scripture, until

you recognize his scent on humanity.

God's Identity Crisis

I AM is not plagued by an identity crisis.

i

wrestle with his character. And in the sweat of discovery find

my own name more sweetly defined by the wildness of my

untamed God.

Gambling Against God

I've drowned in this ocean of odds before, hiding

who I am amongst the smoke and hollow

laughter of the other gamblers,

bluffing my way through disaster.

You know my tell; nothing

is hidden from you.

Attempting to play by my own rules

the hand God dealt, I was swallowed

by a whale.

The House always wins!

Reduced to Prayer

Conversation, smallest unit of trust,

on which faith's DNA is shaped into obedience.

In the garden, heaven multiplies cells of lush truth

while relating to our God.

Willing clay shaped by willing love.

So that when tempted to despair, we are never alone.

Bathe in My Love

My child.

Shake depression's dust from

your travel-beaten soul and bathe in

my pure love. Let me pour my healing fragrance

over your wounds and give you rest.

I plucked you from the orphanage

of death and clothed you in the rich threads

of royalty. Everything I have is yours. I withhold

nothing of myself from you.

I have worn your dust, and known your

sin-beaten sorrow.

I lift your downcast face, to see the

crowning glory of my new day

reflected in the creation of you.

By the Sweat of His Brow

Depression desperately looks for the exits

from the sweat of our nightmares.

You entered our fear-driven world

and sweat blood of understanding

as you stayed, all in, the flesh of our circumstances.

Proving you resurrect us from the terror of our troubles.

Two Stories Diverge

Today we begin composing two books.

Character development starts in your handwriting.

Your life tells a good story.

Fraught with difficulty, but worth sharing.

Do you see your purpose?

How your life encourages others to turn their pages?

Refer back to the gifts and talents

Revealed to you in the first chapters of life.

They foreshadowed the things to come.

As you write this new book, remember:

The hero is never invincible.

He needs others to draw out his character.

There will always be plot twists.

You may even meet an antagonist or two.

Allow them to sharpen who you become.

Your life has always been a page-turner to me.

ABOUT THE AUTHOR

As a survivor of suicide, Karisa saw the need for a raw, passionate, and Christ centered voice in the depression conversation. She began blogging three years ago. Her followers include church leaders, those actively struggling with depression, and fellow grievers. Utilizing her skills as a devotional writer, gift for conversing with readers through poetry, and scriptural insights into the darkness of despair, she listens, encourages, and challenges her readers to find hope amidst depression.

Every story is worth writing!

Become a Page Turner at Karisa's blog, http://www.turningthepageonsuicide.org or follow her on twitter at @moore_karisa. Contact Karisa at turningthepageonsuicide@gmail.com

Made in the USA
Columbia, SC
27 June 2018